ATTRACT MORE CLIENTS, BETTER CLIENTS

The art and science of marketing your business

JON RANDALL, CMC®

ISBN: 1468081446
ISBN 13: 9781468081442

Library of Congress Control Number: 2011962801
CreateSpace, North Charleston, SC

*To my wife, Kathleen; to my sons, James and William;
to my mother and father; to my friend Travis Chaney;
and to all the incredible people I have the privilege
of calling clients. Thank you for believing in me!*

ABOUT THE AUTHOR

Jon Randall is a Certified Master Coach, which is one of the most valued coaching designations recognized by the international business community. He owns a franchise of Ameriprise Financial Services, Inc., which he started in New York in 2000 and moved to North Carolina in 2004. Jon is often a featured national speaker at conferences and events throughout the financial industry. He is a television and radio personality and host of the weekly series *The Jon Randall Show*.

Jon is a transformation guide at Dynamic Directions, along with friend Travis Chaney, CMC, who is the CEO. Together they coach some of the top financial advisors in the country. This group of incredible individuals has inspired Jon to write this book and include many of their best practices.

Jon is also president of Accelerated Coaching, LLC, where he works with business owners, professionals, athletes, and musicians on increasing their emotional intelligence and escalating their level of performance.

The music industry gave Jon a fast start in life and introduced him to the excitement and fulfillment of helping people achieve their dreams. He played drums and percussion while touring the country at a young age, performing in numerous venues, including Carnegie Hall at Lincoln Center, in New York City, and the Hollywood Bowl, in Los Angeles. Jon received his business degree in finance from the University of Massachusetts, Amherst (during the good basketball years!).

Most important to Jon, he is a husband, a dad, a son, a brother, and an uncle. He resides in Greenville, North Carolina, with his family.

TABLE OF CONTENTS

FOREWORD
TRAVIS RAY CHANEY

CFP, CMC, and CEO of Dynamic Directions

Dear Reader,

This book, authored by my friend and colleague Jon Randall, delivers a variety of ideas on how to attract more clients and develop successful marketing plans. One of the first things you need to know is that effective marketing is only one step on the path to building an extraordinary practice. When attracting new high-net-worth clients, you have a very short window of time to capitalize on their interest—probably about forty-eight hours. The further you get from that window, the tougher it is to keep them interested in the experience you provide. One of the more stressful aspects of marketing can be the emotion expressed as, "I feel like I'm not accomplishing much," when instant gratification escapes you.

Jon Randall is a professional who can help you feel, "I am achieving more than I ever thought!" In this book he shares proven ideas on how to articulate your vision and then implement that vision so that your marketing and follow-up strategies flow seamlessly. Jon will work with you to identify obstacles to your vision and create strategies to overcome those challenges. You can attract the client list of your dreams. You will reach your professional goals—and probably more than a few personal ones along the way.

Know this about Jon: first and foremost, he cares about more than the numbers. He has a passion for developing people. He's not motivated by strictly financial results. He witnesses the positive shifts in thinking and behavior. As coaches, we find some of the most rewarding times are the optimistic "awakenings" our clients experience from our work together. These coaching moments are just as important to Jon as increasing marketing results by 500 percent. I know this not only because have I been in the coaching trenches with Jon, but also because we share shovels digging the ditches together. We emphasize behavioral change for entire firms, too, because we know that if we focus on shaping beliefs and enhancing behavior in ways that align with the results the advisor wants, the desired outcomes will happen.

Jon truly cares about the person, not just the results. He's invested in himself, making a huge commitment to additional training and education to best equip himself to fully serve his clients. Jon is a on a path of lifetime learning, a journey you can join by learning and applying the techniques outlined in this book.

A lot of people just want to tell you what to do. They don't understand the beauty of learning to understand for yourself. Jon helps you determine the best way to do things in your own practice and within your own style. He won't quit until you are satisfied. Jon commits himself to our firm's vision every day: building a better life and practice for financial advisors. If you want this for yourself, then enjoy this book and implement everything you can from Jon's expertise.

Travis Ray Chaney, CFP, CMC
CEO of Dynamic Directions, D2—Inc.
www.dynamicdirections-d2.com

THE MAGNETIC
MARKETING MIND-SET

"No pain, no gain" is a popular motivational statement, especially when you are pedaling up a mountain and every muscle in your body begs for a break. Whether you are tackling the French Alps or a monumental business challenge, the goal is in sight, but the journey challenges you mentally and physically.

As a fellow business owner, I have lived through the pains associated with growing a business and striving for the right marketing regimen to add more quality clients to my roster.

What marketing pains have held you back in the past? For me, the pain circled around not attracting enough ideal clients. Early on, I accepted too many clients who were not a great fit. But I was adding new business...*right?*

I convinced myself that the wrong clients were OK simply because they provided new business. Eventually too many of the wrong clients consumed my time. I pedaled furiously while inching forward. Worst of all, I didn't even realize this was happening!

The combined burden of the day-to-day operations of a business plus servicing existing clients can too often derail us from attracting more of the right clients. Having too many clients, especially too many of the wrong clients, left me sucking air at the bottom of the mountain without any hope of making it to the top.

I ignored this situation by focusing on things that were going well with existing clients. This enabled me to ignore the gaping hole in my business: the importance of attracting more clients, better clients. That is the focus of this book.

A pivotal point came on the brink of making a large investment in marketing. I was about to spend five thousand dollars to generate new business with new prospects. Not knowing if I would achieve important results from this *investment* kept me up at night. There was one memorable moment when I started thinking it would be *much* easier *not* to do this! The realization startled me, and I took a look at myself and my business from a different perspective. *I was focused on the obstacle, not the results!*

Recognizing and working through an overwhelming feeling of doubt and uncertainty is one of the differences between winners and losers. Here's a foundational truth that jumpstarted my thinking: success begins with mind-set. What I like to call the *magnetic marketing mind-set* is an optimal way to think about marketing. It comes down to focusing on the right things and interpreting the returns on your investments of money and time. *Is your current mind-set holding you back from bigger results?*

Some define insanity as doing the same thing over and over again and expecting a different result. However, people who try to achieve different results merely by trying different actions obtain limited, short-term, or no results. *Why?* Something greater holds them back—their mind-set.

Too often, there can be a gap in your current mind-set and the magnetic marketing mind-set. Think about what is going on in your head right now. The way we think about situations— whether they are good or bad—can dramatically influence our actions and behaviors. These thought processes build from your experiences in life. This works the same way in both your personal and business life. The mind collects data over time to form your core beliefs. These beliefs are the foundation of your mind-set! People who have a positive mind-set tend to achieve better results than those who have a negative mind-set. *Here's why.* Your actions are constantly influenced by your mind-set. That's one reason you may not attract more high-quality clients. A negative mind-set (and negative self-talk) can drag your business down and repel ideal clients from your business. Consider these examples of a negative mind-set:

I don't think people value what I do.
I can't ask for a referral in this economy.
I can't ask clients for referrals because they will think I'm desperate.
Asking my best clients for referrals might tarnish our relationship.
I am uncomfortable asking for referrals.
Marketing needs to have a silver bullet providing instant results.
I don't have capacity for new clients.
I shouldn't mix my business life and personal life.
I make enough to get by for now.
I don't want to change.

Your mind-set is a critical factor if you hope to achieve results. When I first started my financial planning practice, I devoted most of my work week cold-calling people to acquire new clients. I spent more than thirty hours per week making phone calls from a closet in a large office building in Long Island, New York. Yes, an actual closet, because there was no cubical available. The initial excitement of being in my new business pushed me through the adversity and embarrassment of having people constantly hang up on me.

Many financial advisors around me quickly developed a negative *woe-is-me* mind-set, but I avoided that. Instead I drew on my personal experiences gained when working in the music industry to help me persevere. I told myself, "If I do the right things, good things will happen."

This had worked for me when I started as "the new kid," playing percussion and drums in touring groups. My focus on what I wanted, combined with hard work, helped me close the gap between where I was and where I wanted to be. It was easier to focus on the process—the actions it takes to be successful.

Surely, the same approach was transferable to my new endeavor in the financial industry…or maybe not. Although I avoided a negative mind-set, I eventually noticed negative biases of my own that developed from this new situation.

Successful advisors built their businesses doing this, so I should do it too.
Making phones call until 9:00 every weeknight and every Saturday morning is just what you have to do to make it in this business.

Meanwhile, my creative juices dried up as I slogged along. *My biases boxed in my thinking.* I was stuck completing processes I felt necessary because, *"That's just the way it works."* If I thought of something different, my biases sprang this response on me: *"Oh, no, I can't do that. That will never work."*

This is not so much a negative mind-set, but rather a set of brakes that holds most people back. The brain is most comfortable with routines and habits. When something outside the norm comes up, our brains tell us, *"Wait a minute, that's not what we do around here!"* Ask yourself, *"What are the biases holding me back right now?"*

After many months of phone calls and thousands of people hanging up on me, my mind became numb. Yet I continued to focus on the process. It was a numbers game: a certain number of phone calls yielded a certain number of people I talked to, which in turn led to a chance of them coming into my office for a meeting. It was easy to estimate how many phone calls were needed to achieve the results I wanted. I increased the number of calls I made per week in an effort to exceed my goals.

Now, instead of feeling like I was cycling through the Alps, I felt like I was riding a stationary bike in a windowless gym. One weekend when I was away from the office and my numbed state of mind, I worked out the math behind my approach and the amount of time I was spending. One full year of that approach would equal almost three months of my life per year spent on the phone. *Shocking!*

Finally, I performed another calculation to try to justify such a huge investment of time in cold calls. *The calculation?* I determined that my hourly rate equaled the revenue from the clients acquired from phone calls divided by the hours spent on the phone. *OUCH!* This moment caused a monumental mind-set shift. Never again would I waste such a large investment of unrewarded time in marketing or any other department of my business.

What is the best way to develop a better mind-set to positively influence your results? Don't delay—use the services of a professional coach. Yes, you can work through a mind-set change on your own. However, the people who accomplish a mind-set makeover most quickly and efficiently usually work with a coach. *Need proof?* Ask successful athletes how coaching has helped them! Most professional athletes have similar physical abilities; it is their mind-set and mental conditioning that make the best stand out. This is true in sports, music, business, and other professions.

My first memorable experience of being coached came when I began touring the country and performing music. Colin McNutt is a world-champion individual drummer who works with some of the best percussionists around the world. Colin helped me accelerate my drumming performance abilities years beyond my prior skill level in a matter of months. We did minimal work on how I actually played; mostly Colin tackled my thought processes when drumming.

He helped me uncover the negative mind-sets that held me back. At first, we identified these and became aware they were there. Then Colin helped me see how these negative mind-sets showed up in my performance. Some were basic, but I had overlooked them.

For example, when I felt something was difficult for me to play, I struggled playing and performing that piece. Colin helped me prioritize which negative attitudes held me back the most and limited my results. Working on these small mental attitudes led to massive improvement at a rapid pace! I could not have done this on my own—this is why many athletes have coaches. This was a time in my life when I felt as though I had climbed off the stationery bike and was flying down a hill on a racing bike.

Working on my mind-set with a coach helped me achieve the results I wanted significantly faster than I would have otherwise. For me, coaching results started with music and transferred into business. In both cases my performance got better and better. In business, we perform when we are with clients and prospects. *Do you feel like you have ever been stuck on the stationary bike with your business?*

Coaching is a blossoming industry because it works. There are many versions and varieties of coaching. Don't confuse coaching with consulting! Consulting is about finding solutions and aligning with best practices. Sometimes corporations muddle coaching, consulting, management, training, and development into one word: leadership. This is dangerous because each offers very different things.

Consider my friend and client Steve Felton. He spent two months making a decision about coaching after having already used the expertise of various consultants, managers, and leaders. These were all talented people who had accomplished important tasks for him. But none of them ever really worked on his mind-set—their focus was mostly on tactics. *They worked on his actions to influence his results.*

Finally, he decided to engage with me in a coaching relationship, based on the recommendation of another client. We worked on his mind-set for six weeks. In the following month (Steve's forever memorable June of 2010), his business experienced such explosive growth that he immediately made a profit greater than his entire future investment in our coaching relationship!

"I was in a tough place and became complacent with my business," Steve says. "I ran into a friend of mine in the same industry at a conference who looked unusually happy. When I asked him why he looked so great, he pointed to Jon Randall. 'This guy has changed my life.' After jumping in with Jon, it has been life changing! I am more focused on the right things, and results came quickly. Jon has never blown smoke at me. He has been genuine, listens well, and knows what to say and how to communicate the message. He helped me in ways that others never worked on with me. I now communicate my vision much more effectively to my clients and am getting bigger and better results!"

It's true. Formulating and communicating your vision is vital to success. People work on tactical actions all the time. Don't get me wrong. Tactics are valuable, but there's important work to be done inside the mind first. To me, coaching is about working on the mind and what's going on inside of us. *That's the monumental difference between obtaining mediocre and amazing results.*

Coaching is a process that leads to profound mind-set shifts, which can then lead to changes in your actions that help you achieve more positive results. Coaching needs to come first, before work is done with consultants, managers, trainers, and others. Here's why: working on actions first will lead to small or short-term results—or no results at all. Working on the mind-set first can lead to long-term, sustainable results. This can be a somewhat alien concept for many folks, so try remembering the acronym MARs.

MIND-SET ⟹ ACTIONS ⟹ RESULTS

To see MARs in action, you have to accept some change in your life. Change is one of the most difficult things for human beings to accomplish because the brain relies on routines and habits, both good ones and bad ones. To develop different, long-term, consistent actions to achieve results, you need to change your mind-set. Successful growth-oriented businesses embrace this change.

As you read this book, pay attention to your mind-set. I like to tell people, "Think about what you are thinking about." This simply means to be aware. *Pay attention to what you pay attention to.* When you have more awareness of your thought processes, you can better influence your mind-set, your actions, and ultimately your results.

My mission in life is to help people get where they want to go and beyond faster than they ever thought possible. Take the journey: read this book and apply the principles in your life and your business. *Step down off the stationary bike. Let's take your business to the next level, where you can feel the wind in your face racing down the hills of the Alps!*

CHAPTER 1: MARKETING MINDSET REVIEW

1. Your mind-set has the greatest influence on your results.

2. Seek and destroy your negative mindset and negative self-talk.

3. Recognize the difference between coaching and consulting.

4. Embrace working with a coach and work on your mind-set *first.*

5. Remember MARs (Mindset – Actions – Results).

EXERCISE #1 – MIND-SET MATRIX

Write out your positive and negative mind-sets. Add your positive and negative actions.

POSITIVE MIND-SET	NEGATIVE MIND-SET
POSITIVE ACTIONS	**NEGATIVE ACTIONS**

- *Which of your positive mind-sets have contributed to your success?*

- *Which negative mind-sets will you work on changing first?*

- *How will this change have an impact on your negative actions and ultimately your results?*

WHY DO BUSINESS WITH YOU?

Picture yourself going to your favorite restaurant. There are different levels of experience and value at most restaurants. You can order just a salad and a glass of water. This budget meal yields the least number of visits from the servers. You can add an entrée and a soft drink, which will yield a few more visits from the staff at this middle level. Or you can add appetizers, dessert, and a bottle of wine. This is a higher level, and the staff will be the most attentive, making the maximum number of visits. At this level you might even enjoy a visit from the chef, manager, or owner.

These are three different experiences at the same place of business. Some people want the budget salad and water, and there's value in that. But if you want to bring in more customers similar to your best clients—clients you want to "duplicate"—you need to consider who the best clients are. Which clients do you want more of? Which ones do you want to spend your time with? I've found that too many businesses cater to customers who want the midlevel experience when instead they need to differentiate between their small and large clients. *What does your highest level look like?*

Why do people want to conduct business with you? To discover this answer, you have to fully explore the value you offer people. Try to answer these value questions yourself: *Why should clients value your services? What do you offer that no one else can equal?* Then ask clients why they do business with you and what they value most about you. Their answers will provide essential information for you. Here's why: the importance of working on your clients' experience and the value they receive is to build not only satisfied clients but *client advocates.* Advocates are the clients you like, who like you, and who sing your praises. They are so satisfied with the experience of doing business with you that they can't help but tell others about it.

Here's what client advocates rave about:

- ***Integrity*** tops everyone's list of top values. Integrity is doing what you say you will do. This is a basic of business. You have integrity when you give the client's best interest top priority. When you make a tough decision that is better for your client than it is for your business—that's integrity. People recognize integrity and embrace those who value and demonstrate it. After many years of coaching in the financial industry, I've found that superior financial advisors maintain the highest level of integrity; they always do what is right for the client. Consider this example: a client is interested in a product that pays a high commission. The client heard about this product from someone else. You help by showing that this product is not the best fit for the client's needs. Instead of collecting a high commission, you recommend the right thing for the client. That's integrity.

- **Relationships** provide a foundation for business. To give your client a valued experience you need to focus on your relationship with that client. Connect with your best clients on a personal level. If people get to know you, like you, and trust you, then they do business with you. The more deeply your relationship engages the qualities of integrity and follow-through, the more business you can do with people. Advocates need to develop this level of relationship with you. Talk about things outside of your business relationship. Ask them about the things they value the most—how they are personally or how their family fares. Join in activities with them that you both enjoy outside your business relationship. Some of my best clients and I talk about personal topics more than business topics. This is a sign of a strong relationship.

- **Follow-up** is another key quality in the experience your client has with you. Matt Davenport, my friend and a top attorney, treats all his clients as if it is a privilege to work with them. This provides a contrast with other attorneys who make their clients feel like they are doing a favor in accepting the client's business. Matt attributes much of his success to his timely follow-up with clients and prospects. Once he read an article about a CEO who made it a policy within his firm for all employees to return a phone call, email, or fax with a phone call within one hour of receiving it. That CEO's business increased dramatically. Matt has taken the same approach. Now people talk about the value in their experience of doing business with Matt, and this magnetic marketing attracts more clients.

My own coaching clients receive a written summary of our conversation with highlighted action items as soon as we hang up the phone from our sessions. They are usually surprised by the fast turnaround, and our follow up shows that we care about them and their results.

Clients WILL forget your value! *Be prepared for this.* If you wish to understand this, think about your car. How often do you consider the value of the features that made you purchase your car: the make, color, the comfortable seats, engine components, air conditioning that works in uncomfortable weather, and safety features like airbags? Probably not that often; your car moves you to and from where you want to go. When clients forget your value, it is not because they don't "get" it, but rather it's because they forgot about it just like you forget the features of your car. You need to remind them of your value and help them understand your usefulness more often.

Never attribute your value and your clients' successes to something you have done. Instead, highlight their results and their success as you take them down memory lane. You can uncover occasions when you provided value by simply showing them what they have accomplished. After this type of review, a client who recognizes value might say something like, *"We couldn't have done this without you."* This is code for *"You are valuable to us!"*

At this point you are on your way to building client advocacy. Remind clients of the value of their work with you and help them interpret it in their terms and their perspective—otherwise they WILL forget over time.

Here's the flipside, suggesting another advantage to being alert to your clients' perception of your value. By walking clients through this process you can discover when your value is being overlooked. *This has happened to me before, and I was grateful for the opportunity to remedy my client's impressions.*

One time, a financial planning client questioned my value in one of our interactions. The client was dealing with some personal issues, and he projected his frustration on me. We immediately took a time-out. We discussed all the frustrations and wrote them down. Then we took a walk down memory lane and reviewed where the client was before we started working together, what he had accomplished since we started, and his specific results.

"Oh, I guess I forgot all about this," was the client's comment. We were able to overcome his frustration and find solutions more effectively because there was no longer a value issue.

If you sense you are not being valued by your clients, you need to address this as soon as possible. Letting it linger is like forgetting old milk in the refrigerator; it doesn't take long before it makes everything smell bad. If you don't address this any additional effort on your part will prove pointless. Sometimes people try to do even more for their clients to make them happy. This can make the situation worse—the client knows what is going on.

Take them with you down memory lane and review what the client has accomplished and the results that have been achieved. If you have given good value, it will be easy to turn things around with the client.

Value can be a tough concept to define in the service industry. To help people "interpret" value, you need to bring it to life. If you are reading this book in a chair, you can easily relate to this example. I could sell you a chair and tell you, "This is an extremely nice chair. It sells for four hundred dollars. You will not find a better chair."

This really doesn't matter much to the buyer—what does nice and better mean? To reveal my value, I need to interpret that value from the buyer's perspective. "This chair is made with special leather that is extra thick. Since you mentioned you have children, you'll be glad to know this chair repels stains and scratches." I could then demonstrate this for them. "The leather is soft and comfortable, so after a long day at work and playing with the kids you can settle in to relax. Here, sit down and try it out." Once they are seated, go on. "Since the leather and cushioning is durable, it will last longer than other chairs, which ultimately saves you money in the long run."

Which chair would you buy—the expensive first one or the descriptive second one? I was describing the same chair both times, but the value was interpreted very differently.

Every business sells its services. Some professionals and business owners think they are not in sales when they often are. Yes, surgeons, doctors, attorneys, and accountants—you sell your services too! Properly interpreting value from the buyer's perspective is the difference that lets you the edge over your competition.

Not convinced yet? Many professional athletes have favorite parks they love to play in. What is the difference in value between one park and the next? Growing up in Maryland, my father would take me to Baltimore Orioles baseball games. Memorial Stadium was an old venue with limited nostalgia value and not much more. As a kid, I didn't know the difference—it was simply a huge place where I watched my favorite team and favorite players with my family.

When Camden Yards was built in Baltimore in 1992, it was considered the nicest baseball park in professional baseball. *What a difference!* People wanted to attend more than ever before because there were so many enhancements the old park hadn't offered. Camden Yards offered a better baseball experience. Attendance increased, with not only local fans attending but also people traveling to see the new park. It became a favorite park for the players as well.

Remember my friend Steve Felton? He built an office "ballpark" for his best financial planning clients. His physical office building is beautiful; his team treats everyone like gold; there is always someone answering incoming phone calls (never a machine or phone menu); meetings and interactions with clients are frequent. There are special events for these special clients and they receive gifts that arrive unexpectedly. People talk about Steve's "park" and describe their experience to their friends and colleagues. Most importantly, people talk about how Steve helped them, which is the ultimate reason for the "park."

Another example is Derrick Kinney, ChFC, who is in the top 1 percent of financial advisors nationally. He has also built a "ballpark" where people want to play. The experience begins from the moment clients walk through the door and are greeted immediately and warmly by one or two staff members. Derrick describes the lobby as a "decompression center."

"Clients are coming from a busy day in the office and all of life's other problems," he says. "We want them to relax, feel at home, and feel appreciated. We're very professional but also very family oriented. The goal is when I walk out of my office and greet the client, they should joke about having so much fun out here—'Why do we want to come in and talk with you?!' It's that feeling that the whole team is working on their behalf."

Another area where Derrick excels in communicating his value to clients is through his work with the media, including newspapers, radio, and television stations throughout the country.

"Credibility is very important to communicating value," he says. "One of the things I like to do is work with the media when the opportunity arises. The media wants someone to talk about something in an easy to understand way. Over time, people feel like they already know me when they walk through my door. 'I've heard him talk. I want to make sure he's the same person that I read.' As long as there is a similarity there—hey, he is the same person—they feel comfortable asking, 'Will you take me on as a client?'"

What will persuade people to become a part of your offered experience? Think about the amenities and services people will talk about. Make sure you are clear from the beginning about what you offer so they recognize what your "four-star dining experience" means in terms of value—attention to detail, high quality, and overall experience. Then you can be certain they will tell others about their experience.

CHAPTER 2: MARKETING MIND-SET REVIEW

1. Value Interpretation is vital in business.

2. *Clients WILL forget your value!* Remind them more often.

3. Build your "ballpark" so that people will want to come and play.

4. Make your value clear to clients and prospects; offer different levels of value.

5. Bring this value to life to help attract more people who match your best clients.

EXERCISE #2 - VALUE INTERPRETATION

- *If your clients took a survey about you and your team, what top three items would show up as highly valued about what you do?*

- *How will you effectively communicate your value to clients and prospects?*

- *How can you encourage your clients to communicate this value to others?*

TARGETED MARKETING: A WIDE NET DOESN'T ALWAYS CATCH A BIG FISH

In marketing, much as in fishing, casting a wide net is not always as effective as using a specific bait on a special hook. It all depends on what you hope to land.

If your goal is to catch large tuna, then you have to consider what will best lure them, their individual feeding habits and preferred bait, the water depth, and the ideal temperature where they swim.

When you don't consider those specifics you might catch an occasional tuna, but you'll also catch other fish that take up room in your boat but aren't what you were fishing for. If you are trying to catch large tuna, do you really want the other fish?

A net catches many different things including garbage in the sea. Specific bait helps you target what you are fishing for. Are you casting a net hoping for the best or are you targeting what you want using the appropriate bait?

Mass advertising can be too wide a net for some businesses. Instead of enticing targeted high-quality clients, it appeals to a larger spectrum and catches less desirable fish. Why is this not effective? Mass advertising creates additional awareness, but it doesn't always lead directly to new customers and clients.

I have seen businesses essentially set their money on fire with mass advertising, burning up thousands! "That's what we do around here," is the internal message. They just do it because they believe that is what they are supposed to do. If you are making consistent and significant profits using mass advertising then good for you, go for it. *But my guess is this is not you.* If there aren't measurable results from your efforts, stop wasting time and money. Change the bait!

Remember my epiphany about the futility of cold calls in the early years of my financial practice? Once I started to change my mind-set, I thought the next step was to find the most successful advisors in the area and determine what processes they used to grow.

The first three individuals I spoke with all said the same thing worked for them—seminars. These are educational programs presented over dinner in which you speak about different topics. Seminars allow you to connect with people in the audience. I said to myself, *"I can do this too!"* I learned everything there was to know about seminars; this basically consisted of purchasing a list of prospects and inviting them to dinner. This list was filtered to include only optimal candidates.

This was casting my net in a targeted way, right? Well, yes and no. As I did more and more dinner seminars, I acquired more clients, which justified continuing to do more seminars. I became one of the top seminar marketers in the country and was a highly sought after speaker at these events. Other financial advisors and marketing professionals started to come to me to find out what I was doing that was working so well.

Again, this was a great way to leverage my time. I talked to many people all at once instead of making thousands of phone calls. Not being a seasoned business owner at that point, I did not calculate profits and losses on a regular basis. Then a business coach helped me think through my marketing investments. Yes, there were good profits from my seminar endeavors, but not to the degree I thought.

One thing the world's top fishermen know is that if you aren't catching the right fish, then it's time to switch the bait. This is easier said than done when you are out in the ocean of marketing trying to determine what bait will reel in quality clients.

Clearly there was more mind-set work ahead for me. The weekend following my coaching session I went out with my wife and some friends. During an evening filled with relaxation and laughter, something profound happened. One of the people I had been getting to know over the previous few months told me that he heard I was doing well with my business and was working hard. The next question gave a jump-start to my marketing evolution. My companion needed my services and wanted to work with me *because he knew me*.

While this may seem like a fundamental truth now, my business radar had been turned completely off in personal settings. This was someone who came to me—I did not pursue him! A month later, a similar situation occurred.

I was just starting to lean to the right side of the laws of attraction. This effect comes into play when people start gravitating to you. It is like a paper clip clinging to a magnet; a mysterious force develops. It is not you pursuing clients, it is you turning on your personal magnet and allowing them to come to you. This force is strongest when there is a personal connection with someone and they sense value in what you do.

At this point, I chose to abandon most of my old marketing strategies. I worked with a coach to further develop my mind-set and my approach to marketing, which accelerated my results. I'm not an isolated case, either. Many top professionals in our field have learned how to become better "fishermen" through their work with a coach.

Someone I had the privilege of helping cast the right bait (and throw away the old net) was Trevor Shakiba, CFP, CRPC, AAMS, from Houston, Texas. Within six months of coaching, Trevor grew his financial planning practice by 50 percent. Much of this was due to a niche he had developed with certain existing clients. Most of our interactions involved identifying and developing effective bait to catch more and better clients.

Trevor spent time with clients and prospects from a focused group of people. He now attracts very affluent clients because he swims in their waters. Trevor is there—they know, like, and eventually do business with him. Together we found ways to do more with his existing fish. We also located the best waters and bait to catch more of the fish he wanted.

"Jon's outside perspective allowed me to think about things differently," Trevor says. "He works with folks who are already where I want to be. He acts as a sounding board, encourager, and he holds me accountable. He also advises in a way that encourages you to make the ultimate decision through reason."

I reviewed and dissected Trevor's client list with him. We brainstormed where else he could go fishing and what bait might work best. Bottom line? The methods we used to attract clients require time, energy, and money; a focused marketing approach creates efficiency in all three areas. Trevor and I were able to accomplish that focused marketing approach in our work together. *Do you want to be the one casting a wide net and catching everything from bluegills on up? Or do you want to attract a specific type of trophy fish—a high-quality client?* My own first focused marketing involved two lists: top prospects to attract and top clients to duplicate. Let's look more closely at the first classification. Top prospects are people you know who would make top clients. Top prospects can also be people you would like to know who would make great clients. Top clients include your most profitable business relationships and the ones you enjoy the most. Make sure your marketing method lines up with what these prospects value.

My second list was called "top clients to duplicate." Duplicating your best clients starts with both a focused mind-set and a process that works for you and your business. Sometimes businesses drop subtle hints to clients saying they are accepting new clients. The hint is almost like a pin dropping. It's there, but just barely perceptible.

Others make it clear to their best clients that they want to work with more people like them. Being direct should not be mistaken with pushing or pursuing. Instead, look at being direct as making your intentions clear. It is like listening to the highest quality piano in a concert hall. *Are you a pin or a piano?*

Knowing your value and identifying that value to your existing clients is the first step in duplicating your best clients. Take time together to review your relationship. Remember to summarize their accomplishments that have occurred during your work with them. It's that walk down memory lane that provides the reminder.

The next step is finding out if your best clients are open to helping you. Let them know they are favored clients (they may not know) and that you would love to work with more people "just like them." Some people prefer not to give referrals—probably about 20 percent of your clients on average. This attitude shouldn't be taken as an insult. It just means that's one less person to focus on for duplication. When you come across these people, don't act offended and don't push the conversation. Simply leave the door open by saying, "don't keep me a secret," and move on.

Identifying candidates can be challenging for some people. Occasionally, clients might need extra help identifying what makes them great clients. Others might need prompts to help them recognize who they know who would be a good fit. If they are really open to helping you connect with others, take time to brainstorm together. Find out more about what they do for business and pleasure and who they know. Let them guide you to your next client. Once you identify potential candidates, find out the best way for you to connect.

A word of advice here: stop giving out business cards. You might have more fun lighting them on fire. Instead, *create future interactions.* How about a business meeting? Perhaps your client talks with the prospect and obtains permission for you to talk with that person directly. What about a joint meeting with the client and the prospect...a casual gathering, a meal, or just coffee?

Many professionals will stop here, *but an incomplete process leads to incomplete results.* While it's a start, you won't attract fish by merely being in the right area. Work behind the scenes to find out what your clients are saying about you. It is easier to understand what more transactional businesses do. Some professionals, like attorneys, have different specialties. Some titles carry baggage, like *financial advisor,* which some people associate with getting sold something. Manage these perception shifts before your client talks to anyone else. If they have trouble knowing what to say, help them build a story with the answers to these three questions:

- *What was it like before we started working together?*

- *Why did you choose me?*

- *What have you accomplished since we started working together?*

The last step is to identify for your clients what will happen next. Make it easy for them to connect you with others. Find ways to assist in the process without making anyone feel uncomfortable. Here's one example: Have your client speak to the prospect within the next week. Then, before you do anything else, follow up with the client to see how the potential connection went.

Five-Step Elite Client Duplication Conversation (VALUE):

Value current clients' recognition of your efforts.
Ask if they will help you.
List candidates and identify potential ways to connect.
Uncover what they will say about you.
Expect a genuine effort.

Marketing can be a targeted process that reaps results. Don't let your net become clogged with fish you aren't interested in and can't do much with. Instead, do your research and target exactly what type of client you want to add to your client roster. Once you've achieved success, work to duplicate those clients.

CHAPTER 3: MARKETING MIND-SET REVIEW

1. Mass advertising doesn't lead to the best results; it only creates awareness.

2. Targeting opportunities allows for better results and faster results.

3. Build lists of your top clients and top prospects.

4. Use the VALUE conversation model to duplicate your best clients.

EXERCISE #3 – ELITE CLIENT AND PROSPECT EXERCISE

- *Who are your favorite clients? Do they know they are your favorite clients?*

- *Which clients generate the most revenue?*

- *Are there clients who show up on lists of both favorite clients and highest revenue generators?*

- *What do these people have in common? Can you find a possible niche?*

- *How would you describe your elite Client?*

WHO ARE YOUR CONNECTORS?

*I*sn't it interesting how some people "have a guy" for everything? They love connecting others and always have the name of someone you can connect with. One of my favorite connectors is my friend Mike Mullis, from North Carolina. He is the type of person who, in casual conversation, will throw in a recommendation. He likes saying, *"You've got to go see my guy. Tell him 'Mike sent you,' and they will take care of you."* I trust him because, time after time, he has connected me with the right people.

Now, Mike genuinely likes connecting people. He truly enjoys helping people find what they are looking for and being the one who helps them connect to the right people. Mike doesn't connect people for kickbacks or commissions, he connects them because he cares and wants the people he knows to be taken care of.

"I do enjoy seeing people have success," Mike says. "Success begets success. The more successful I can help people to be, the more successful I feel. Hey, if everyone around me is benefiting—it will ultimately benefit me."

This is a key quality to remember with connectors. *They enjoy making connections*—so help them do it more often. Be intentional about communicating to them their value as a connector to you. Sometimes they don't even recognize they are connectors in a formal sense. Mike adds:

"The whole connector thing—I've never looked at it that way. Credibility is in whom you align yourself with. When you have a guy like Jon—who in our area is the best at what he does—it's only natural that if I'm going to help take care of the financial futures of my clients then Jon Randall should be a part of it."

Like Mike, a connector doesn't have to be the mayor of your town. Connectors are simply the people who continually align you with others (i.e., new clients). A connector could be an existing client "who gets it," another professional in a related field, or even someone outside of your practice who is in a position to connect you.

Remember my original mind-set had a gap regarding connecting with people I knew from my personal and social life? *Many professionals have this same issue.* Here's the take-home concept: It is OK to ask your friends, family, clients, and colleagues to connect you with others. If in doubt, ask them if they are comfortable doing so. If they say no, assure them you will never bring this up with them again. If the answer is yes, or their track record as a successful connector is clear, make it easier for these people to connect people to your business.

Consider this example that occurred with some clients I considered some of my best. They didn't produce the highest amount of revenue, but they were enjoyable to work with. When they showed up on my appointment calendar, I really looked forward to seeing them. Over time, they talked to people about my services. As a result I acquired many new clients through them. Unfortunately, I lost the right perspective concerning their connecting skills.

Remember MARs? Mind-set—Action—Results. Well, my mind-set went something like this: *"These people have sent me so many new clients, and they have been so good to me. I don't feel like I can go back to that well. I don't want to appear greedy."* This attitude held me back! One of my coaches helped me identify how these clients were among my most valuable because of their ability to *easily connect me* with others. I had never thought of it this way.

In the next meeting with these enjoyable clients, I shared with them my belief that they were some of my best clients because I looked forward to our meetings and because they had connected me with so many other clients. *They were shocked and flattered!* We took a trip down memory lane and reviewed all the people they had connected to me. I told them I wanted to do something special with them as a thank you, and I would pick up the tab.

We planned a fun outing filled with activities we all enjoyed. The week before our outing, they called to tell me their best friends were coming into town for the weekend. *I assumed our outing was off.* Instead, they asked if they could bring their friends along. They offered to pay for their friends, and at that moment the light bulb went off for me!

"The more the merrier!" I said, and indicated I was still picking up the tab. It turned out that the friends had been hearing about me through my client. *Mostly about our connection and not as much about the business we did together.* Within one month, the friends became new clients.

I called the clients who referred them to see what they thought of the "thank you" gift I sent them for aligning yet another client with me. They said they had such a fun evening that they would be open to inviting others to join in next time. We brainstormed about activities to do and people they could invite. These people "got it"—they helped me connect with people who had similar interests. My number of new clients doubled that year.

Your connectors are the easiest place to go for new clients. These people have successfully connected you to a new client in the past; make it easy for them to do it again.

Sometimes it is hard for clients to recognize potential candidates for you to connect with. Let's face it, most people don't know specifics about their friends' finances; respect for privacy may prevent them from knowing how much they earn, how much they have in their 401(k) plan, if they have a will, who does their tax returns, or what vendors they use for their businesses. However, it is easy for clients to know who likes the activities or hobbies that you like.

Maybe you have a favorite restaurant, an interest in music, a passion for golf or a sports team, travel, cooking, gardening, shopping, fishing, or some other pastime. Find ways to connect with people on levels that you both enjoy. Leverage your connectors to help you. I promise you that they get it—or they wouldn't have started connecting you with their friends and colleagues in the first place!

Here are some other connector possibilities. Professional alliances can be powerful connectors for your business. Some estate-planning and elder-law attorneys obtain most of their new clients from financial planners. Some financial advisors receive most of their new clients from CPAs. Some medical professionals land most of their clients from other medical professionals. Maximize these relationships!

Professionals can reward connectors in different ways. One top financial advisor I work with rewards connectors for sending referrals before their referral even has a chance to become a new client—he sends them to the Starbucks next to his office for their favorite indulgence. If a person they referred to the practice becomes a client, the advisor rewards the connector at a higher level. This can include a customized gift, taking the connector out to do something special, or celebrating with the connector and the referral.

In many industries there are regulations and restrictions regarding giving gifts for referrals. These can vary by state. Protect yourself and your business by checking into the fine print before you decide what type of reward makes sense and is appropriate. Once you do your homework, find out what your connectors like or enjoy doing. This can help you determine the best reward to encourage their helpful behavior.

The networking principles coming up in chapter 5 will be important as you consider connectors and other professionals linked to your business. Other professionals can be difficult to turn into connectors. One reason? Because others in your line of business are already trying to score referrals from them! One CPA from New York City told me he receives an average of twenty phone calls per day from financial advisors wanting to connect with him. You will find this with many professionals. My team plays gatekeeper, protecting my business from those trying to connect with my clients through me. They keep them away like the guards of a palace keep out assassins. You will run into this too. *Will you get lost in the crowd and be blocked or will you stand out and get in with the others you want to connect with?*

Professionals don't want to refer you! Something bad might happen that would reflect back negatively on the professional. What if a CPA referred someone to a financial advisor and the client lost money? This is one of the risks a CPA sees and is usually a top reason why they will not easily refer clients. This can be a mountain to challenge your skills. You must prove your value and make your professional connectors look good to their clients. If you can create a mutually beneficial situation in which both you and the professional are able to help a client, everyone wins. Try to coordinate joint meetings during which you and the professional meet with someone together.

Don't keep score of how many referrals you have given someone else. The relationship with a professional should be about helping others and offering value. Give them reasons to refer to you. Solicit their feedback regarding solutions you offer that can make them look good. Be specific when providing details, and use these solutions to identify specific people you can go to together.

Be creative and discover how your favorite clients and professionals can become even more helpful as connectors for your practice. Don't forget to be intentional about being a connector in your own right. I love connecting people with a service they need, as long as I know there is value and they will be taken care of. I connect my financial planning clients to attorneys and CPAs so that they receive quality services, and I connect my coaching clients to other businesses that will be helpful to them.

If you had a hen that laid golden eggs, how would you treat it? Treat your connectors the same way. Make sure they feel appreciated, even rewarded. They could be the greatest assets to promote your business growth!

CHAPTER 4: MARKETING MIND-SET REVIEW

1. Connectors are the people who help feed you clients.

2. Identify your connectors and take care of them!

3. Spend more time with your connectors and treat each one like your best client *even if a connector isn't a top client.*

4. Find more ways for these people to connect you. It is OK to go back to the well.

EXERCISE #4 – CONNECTOR EXERCISE

- *Who has referred new clients to you?*

- *Who has referred you multiple new clients?*

- *How have you shown your appreciation?*

- *What will you do differently to take greater care of these people going forward?*

The Art of Meeting People and Networking

Baseball great Cal Ripken, Jr., was my hero growing up, and he still is today. He worked hard and maintained a superior attitude—attributes that were important to me even at a young age. I clearly recall one rain-soaked game in the 1980s when the Baltimore Orioles were losing badly but Cal was still diving for the ball in the mud as if it was a close championship game. The day I had the chance to meet Cal in person and ask for his autograph...he was so much taller than I had imagined! He looked me in the eyes and smiled as if my twelve-year-old self was an important person. He shook my hand, signed his autograph, and offered some inspirational words of wisdom—"keep working hard." *This was such a positive experience for me, one I've never forgotten.*

You make lasting impressions on others every day, too. People develop an opinion about you on a subconscious level before you ever say a word. Pay attention and manage these initial impressions when you meet people. This is important not only in business, but also in personal settings. Here are some practical things you can do to connect with positive energy right from the start.

Typically the first thing that happens when we meet someone is a handshake. *Don't underestimate the importance of this!* There are many components to the handshake that I work on with the professionals I coach and consult with. The specific items we work on are based on many different positive and negative experiences.

Here is an example of how a famous handshake can go wrong. My wife and I, along with some of her family, had the opportunity to meet Mayor Michael Bloomberg of New York City. As this event approached, I helped her family realize that this was not just the mayor, but a highly successful billionaire businessman I looked up to.

After we met him, I walked away with my wife, discussing how neat it was to meet someone of Mayor Bloomberg's caliber. Behind us, one of my wife's brothers commented, "He was bogus." I stopped, turned around and said, *"What?"* Kevin explained that Mayor Bloomberg gave a "dead fish" handshake, indicating he did not care about us. He was right—this was bogus! To this day, many years later, Mayor Bloomberg is infamously known as "dead fish handshake guy" among my wife's family, not as "the successful billionaire and successful mayor."

At the other end of the spectrum, a strong handshake can inspire a positive and lasting first impression. Ameriprise Financial executive vice president Bill Williams looks people in the eyes, smiles and executes a perfect handshake. When I met Bill in person for the first time, I instantly had a very positive impression of him. *He did not have to say anything to create this, it just happened.*

Whole books could be written on the details and nuances associated with the all-important handshake! Non-verbal communication can be significantly more powerful than verbal communication. *This is an important element for the professionals I work with who want to attract new customers and clients.*

Consider these questions from Bill Williams as you make that first impression.

"Are you looking them in the eye when you have that first hello? What things do you choose to talk about and who do you talk about?" Bill cautions: "Don't spend the first interaction talking about yourself. Ask questions. Invite conversation with open-ended questions. Those are some of the things people can do to make themselves more approachable and make that first impression a better one."

After the initial handshake, you enter into a conversation. *Let people talk about their favorite subject—themselves!* Always remember, it's about the potential client, not you. This elevates your new friend's comfort level. Conversational models and specific questions to ask are also key elements for the professionals I work with.

Think about a person who has drawn you out and made you feel like the only person in the room during a conversation. *How did you view that person afterward?* Chances are they asked you seemingly casual questions. Have questions ready that can generate conversation and allow people to talk about their favorite subject—themselves. If someone tries to turn the conversation back to you, give a quick response and turn it back around to them.

People do business with those they know, like, and enjoy being around. As contrary as it sounds, people feel like they know and like you if you engage them in talking about their own experiences. There is a subconscious joy to this. They will remember talking to you and will relate that feeling of joy to you. Facilitate this delight and you will attract more people to you.

One evening, my wife and I conducted an experiment based on this strategy. After speaking at an event in San Francisco, I extended the trip with my wife (no kids this time!) for a long weekend. After touring some wonderful wineries on our first day, we dined that evening at an exquisite French restaurant just north of Napa. The tables were small and situated close to one another. It was almost as if we were all sitting together, similar to restaurants in New York City. To make the best of the close quarters, we engaged the couple at the table next to us. We decided beforehand that when either of us talked, we could only ask questions and not talk about ourselves. To avoid being rude, we could answer a question asked of us, but then we had to turn it back around with a question to them.

A man and woman sat at the first table next to us; not a couple, just two people traveling together on business. With the man sitting next to me and the woman sitting next to my wife, it was only natural they engaged us individually. My wife and I were not aware of each other's conversations. When the two left, they said we were the nicest people they had ever met, and they had the best time at dinner. This made us each smile because they didn't know anything about us! My wife was puzzled yet amazed.

The next evening we did the same thing again, for fun, at a famous Japanese restaurant in Napa. We got the same reactions, only from a husband and wife this time. They wanted to follow up with us and have dinner again on our next trip. We said nothing about ourselves; we only asked questions. We facilitated the joy of letting people talk about their favorite subject—themselves. *If you have never done this before, start now.* If you are already engaging others in this way, keep working at it. This is a great area to work on with a coach and consultant if you hope to acquire new clients.

Finding connections is a natural extension of talking with people. You can reach a high level of comfort with people by talking about something you know the other person relates to. Direct your questions toward something you both have in common. This could include shared associates, vacationing or traveling to the same place, growing up in a similar area, or enjoying the same sport or team.

Networking encourages connections across the spectrum. Think of networking as the "brackish water" of business and personal connections. Brackish water is a mix of fresh water and salt water found where the two meet, as when a river connects to an ocean. Both salt and sweet are present simultaneously, blending. Remember, people do business with those they know and those they like. You are not crossing forbidden barriers if you talk about personal things with the people you do business with (or with the people you would like to do business with).

As you meet key people, find more ways to follow up. Attend an event together; enjoy a meal, or simply have a cup of coffee and talk about something you have in common. Chapter 7 offers additional follow-up ideas, but remember that the goal is to attract, not pursue.

Networking with other professionals is a similar process. They, too, will respond positively to the networking principles you use in your personal life. When, after you have given them the opportunity to talk about themselves, you are offered a chance to talk about what you do, it is important to set yourself apart.

There are terms used within every industry and business that mean something to you but nothing to others. The financial industry offers a perfect example. *What is a financial advisor, exactly?* An investment broker, insurance agent, mortgage broker, loan officer, or even a bank teller? The legal arena is another area where roles can be easily confused. Attorneys can focus on estate planning, wills, trusts, divorces, patents, corporate law, criminal representation, as well as many other forms of specialization.

In your own relationships, avoid this kind of language: *I am a financial advisor, and I focus on financial planning.* You might know what that means, but others don't! Some people think financial planning is simple investing, while others, including you, have different definitions. I call this "advisor speak." We financial advisors are notorious in the financial industry for using terms that mean something to us but not the same thing to others! This confusion can only detract from your overall impression. Eliminate your industry-only terms; use more universal language.

Be intentional about the language you use with others. One preparation tip is to think through or even write your story down—without using industry terms. *This is something I often work on with professionals.* Some top financial planners use analogies to sports and coaches. They compare what they do with the way a head coach helps athletes reach desired goals. Some top estate attorneys make analogies to building a ship and launching it. People can relate to these images easily. You can also share a motivational story of how you were able to help a particular client. Be sure to add how those types of relationship create the most satisfaction and enjoyment within your business.

This relational method might take longer if your services are more in-depth. For those in transactional professions such as property insurance agents, real estate agents, and traffic law attorneys, it is easier and faster for people you meet to gravitate towards you and do business. Someone in a more in-depth and engaged service, like a true financial planner, takes longer to attract people, since there is a higher level of trust involved to do business. *Don't be discouraged if it takes time to attract your major clients!* Stay with them and continue to interact. Learn their stories; find common ground, and then share your expertise with them.

Remember—you don't have to be Cal Ripken, Jr., (or Mayor Bloomberg) to leave a memorable impression with people. You do need to be in the moment, however, with a deliberate focus on the other person. Listen and note what's important to those you connect with. That bit of attention will make all the difference in your future interactions.

CHAPTER 5: MARKETING MIND-SET REVIEW

1. First impressions last a long time. Manage your first impression to keep it positive and engaging. Above all, avoid the "dead fish" handshake!

2. Don't repel people with negative nonverbal communications.

3. It's not about you; it's about *them*! Connect through questions and let others talk about their favorite subject — themselves.

4. Find things you have in common and position your questions to go further in this direction.

5. Sound different from others in your industry by avoiding industry terms.

6. Use stories and analogies so people can more easily relate to you and what you do.

EXERCISE #5 – NETWORKING CHEAT SHEET

- *What negative nonverbal signals do you need to eliminate from your appearance?*

- *What industry-only terms do you need to eliminate from your language?*

- *Write and memorize three questions to ask people when you meet them.*

- *Write an analogy or story that helps others understand what you do without using industry terms.*

The Difference Between Wow! and Oh

My team held an event for some coaching clients at the Ritz Carlton, in New Orleans, a few years ago. My wife and I arrived a few days early for some vacation time. Just after checking in, the bellman, who took our bags to our room, happened to be in the elevator with us.

"What are you in town for?" he asked politely. "A business meeting," I said. "But we want to enjoy the city for a few days before it starts."

Then he asked if we were spending the extra time because of any special occasions. My wife mentioned that my birthday was in a few days. The bellman asked if we needed directions or any recommendations for our destination. We didn't, as we had been there before. We politely finished the conversation and went out to enjoy the day.

That night, when we returned to our room, there was a wrapped gift on the bed with a card. The card read "Happy birthday, Mr. Randall! We are so happy you are staying with us." The gift was a set of four very nice glasses etched with fleurs-de-lis. We still use them today. Every morning I see them when I drink my orange juice and think about the Ritz Carlton and our trip to New Orleans. When we use those glasses with company, I always tell this story, and the response is always what mine was that evening in New Orleans: *Wow!* Based on this experience, I can tell you exactly where we will be staying on our next trip to New Orleans!

When people have an extraordinary experience, they often say *Wow!* The experience was extraordinary and unique—set apart from the norm. Think about an exceptional experience you've had at a place where you do business.

Every time my wife and I stay at a Ritz-Carlton resort, we say Wow! at least once during our stay. Fine dining establishments can elicit the same response. Many people will pay a premium to experience that sort of excellence. The Ritz-Carlton can cost almost ten times more than other valued hotel chains. But then, Godiva chocolates are almost twenty times more expensive than Hershey's chocolates. People want to say Wow! and enjoy an extraordinary experience.

Any time a client says Wow! in my office, my team members look at me and smile. They know their diligent work to eliminate create excitement has paid off. We were intentional about the visual appearance of our brand new office building with palm trees. We decided how neat and clean it would be; the comfortable leather couches in the conference room; the fifty-two-inch flat-screen TV mounted on the wall so that clients can see what we are talking about instead of reviewing a printed piece of paper that is hard to read. We planned to have a client's favorite beverage and snack served to them because we know what it is and exactly how they take their favorite brand of coffee.

But that's only the beginning. In my practice, the Wow! means going the extra step beyond what we said we were going to do. We follow up in a timely manner and keep clients informed on everything. We work to deliver a level of service unparalleled by anything the client has experienced in the past: handwritten notes, special events, surprise gifts, and services that provide an extra level of attention.

For example, handwritten notes have become a lost art form. A handwritten note comes across differently than an email or text message. The extra effort is special for the recipient. I write four handwritten notes each day. Some are for people who do new business with me; others are for a person who sends me a new client or for people who have something positive or negative going on in their lives. The biggest Wow! comes when people receive random notes that are not attached to any of those above listed situations—a "just-because note." *Try it and see what response you get!*

My notes are not lengthy and do not take much time: they are two to three sentences on heavy paper stock with my name at the top. The content of the note is not the main emphasis—the gesture behind the note is the point. Some of my notes simply read: *"Steve, You are doing such a phenomenal job, and I just wanted to let you know how proud I am to know you. Keep up the great work. I look forward to our upcoming interactions, Jon."*

Hand written notes are one of the easiest and most effective ways to stay connected and provide a Wow! moment. My coach sends me "out of the blue" notes. I have received handwritten notes from favorite businesses that I consider tops in their industry. These notes make me feel special—like an important customer, which is always a positive feeling.

Of course there are other ways to create an outstanding experience. Brent Trentham, CFP, is one of *Barron*'s top one thousand financial advisors in America. He cares so much for his clients and gives them such a positive experience that he goes with his top clients to their meetings with other professionals, which has created a Wow! for not only the client but also for the other professionals! The extra service makes a difference.

"Going to meetings with clients began with this thought: how can I ultimately make the clients' lives easier and at the same time help them to ultimately implement some of my recommendations?" says Brent Trentham. "It was those tasks that sometimes clients just don't get around to, like meet with an estate planner or CPA. The first thing I found when I sat in on those meetings is that the client is much more comfortable with me there. I become the mediator or translator, and they tend to be less intimidated by the situation."

There was an extra benefit to the strategy as well. As he attended client meetings with their lawyers and CPAs, those professionals wondered who Brent was and admired the level of attention he paid his clients. He adds: "It's turned out to be a wonderful marketing tool! I didn't do it with that thought in mind, but my presence there created an opportunity there for me as well."

How many financial advisors go with their clients to purchase a car, refinance their mortgage, or organize their estate planning documents in one place? Not many, but the ones who do will enjoy a Wow! response. To the client, the top experience may be an "out of the blue" phone call just to say, "I was thinking of you and wanted to check in and see how you were doing today." These calls appear random, but are actually intentional—preplanned behind the scenes.

The opposite of the Wow! experience is the Oh. Pay attention when you hear an Oh because people remember and talk about the Oh long after a Wow! has passed from memory. When I was new in my practice, I failed to update people when changes were made with new business opportunities. I knew what was going on, but I hadn't learned to consider things from the clients' perspective yet. I started receiving voice mails asking "What is going on with the new thing we are doing?" Once I explained, they would say "Oh." And "I just didn't know what was going on since I didn't hear from you."

Expectations have a lot to do with the Oh. If you don't meet someone's expectations, it leads to an Oh. If you exceed their expectations, that starts to lead to a "Wow!" When someone judges another person or slips in a derogatory comment, this can make you think "Oh." about that person—that type of behavior was not what you expected.

We've all experienced an Oh moment. When you fly first class you expect to be treated at a certain level. You are there because you travel a lot and have been upgraded, used extra miles to upgrade, or paid significantly more than coach to have the extra room and service. When I am in business attire, especially after speaking at a conference or event, I am always treated well. When I am dressed casually, this is not always the case, and it always gives me an Oh moment.

On occasion, I have been completely ignored on a flight because I am casually dressed. I am the last to be asked for a drink and which meal I want to order. The attendants forget to hang my jacket until after they have hung everyone else's. When this happens, I don't want to fly on that airline.

Have you ever gone to a restaurant people are raving about? You have high expectations going in. When the service is slow to your table and not attentive during the meal, this can ruin your experience. The restaurant did not live up to your expectations. Some business owners will chalk up an Oh to a one-time mishap or, worse, they blame the Oh on the client. That is a dangerous approach because it is you, not the client, who controlled the situation. Identify the Oh in your business and eliminate it.

Other examples of the Oh include not following up with people in a timely manner, impolite greetings, phone system menu madness instead of a real live person on the phone, not saying "please" and "thank you." That first physical impression remains crucial as well. Avoid a dirty or unorganized appearance of people or surroundings.

Look at your business from your customer's perspective and identify your current and potential Ohs and eliminate them. For us, the ultimate Wow! comes from the surprise gifts we send to our best clients. They are extras and show people we care about them. They are not expensive or extravagant gifts—just thoughtful ones that last. When they look at these gifts, our clients know that Jon Randall and his team care about them.

In today's high-tech society, there are more opportunities than ever to use social media to create a positive impression. People use the internet every hour of every day. This access offers an excellent way to keep your name in front of people. I have pre-written "touch" emails that go out every month. These offer small tidbits of value for clients and prospects. For me, the point is not so much the content of the emails; it is that my name appears in a client's email inbox. I want them to think of me when they receive it.

An old friend started sending me weekly emails two years ago, when he started his new business. I have yet to read one, but every time they show up in my inbox, I think of this person. When I require his services, I can tell you he will be the first one I call, because he is at the top of my mind.

Take a moment and consider who your prospects think of first when they need your type of services. *Will it be you or someone else?* There are so many social media venues that work to keep your name in front of clients and prospects. Post about upcoming conferences or events, your travel destinations, a win-win you experienced with a client, and similar events and topics. The key is to keep your name in front of people—but do make the content relevant and interesting. Avoid a description of the mundane activities we all go through. Instead, post blurbs that will make others think, "Wow, that person is really interesting."

High Point University, in High Point, North Carolina, provides the ultimate Wow! experience among universities. Dr. Nido Qubein has transformed the way the campus looks and the experience that greets the students and parents. The first time I visited the campus for a workshop with Dr. Qubein, I caught myself continually saying Wow! One of the top positions at the university is the Director of "Wow!" This role is designed to continually provide EXTRAordinary experiences and eliminate any Oh.

The workshops I have attended in High Point are always in an incredible facility that seems like a Fortune Five Hundred company executive building. Just going through the door was a Wow! One day at the first 10:30 break, people made phone calls and visited the rest rooms. One participant used the stall with a door in the men's room. He came out looking slightly disturbed. The Director of Wow happened to be in the rest room at the same time and asked if everything was OK.

"Oh, I'm fine," he said. "It's just that there was no hook on the door to hang my coat." Something amazing happened—hooks were installed in every bathroom stall by lunchtime that day.

Wow! indeed.

CHAPTER 6: MARKETING MIND-SET REVIEW

1. People will say "Wow!" when they have an extraordinary experience.

2. Many people will pay a premium for Wow!

3. The Oh can speak louder than a Wow!

4. Work to anticipate and eliminate the Oh before clients notice them.

EXERCISE #6 – WOW EXPERIENCE

- *When do you hear an Oh, how can you eliminate it?*

- *What are your potential Oh items to eliminate?*

- *What strategies bring out a Wow! in your business?*

- *If you charged fifty dollars for entry to your place of business to get access to purchase your goods in the same way Disney World does, what would it have to be like to justify the entry fee? The answers are the path to WOW!*

AN INVITATION
TO SUCCESS

Y ou want to add more high-quality clients to your business. But it's not as simple as merely extending an invitation. Nothing affects the success of your client acquisition strategies more than your preparation. It is the same for a championship team preparing to win the big game. Practice doesn't make perfect; practice makes permanent. Don't limit your potential for success by being unprepared or boxed in by the same routine because "that's how we always have done these events."

Many businesses hold regularly scheduled events to attract new clients. Just holding events doesn't guarantee success, however. Here's the mind-set we're after: You will not acquire new clients at events; you can only set yourself up for the *opportunity* to acquire new clients in the future. Once you have established that the goal of marketing events is to create opportunities to acquire clients, then you can start building events that work for you.

What will people want to do? Where would people want to go? You need to put yourself in your clients' and prospects' shoes to answer this. A "business" gathering can intimidate some people who are anticipating "the sale." You can ease people's comfort level by connecting in an activity and a place that everyone enjoys.

Here is one of my favorite examples of thinking outside the box for an event that captures a person's attention. Financial advisor Chris Murphy loves going to rock concerts. For one event, he rented a limousine and invited one of his best clients to come along. He told the client to bring along a friend or two. The group went, enjoyed the concert, and had a great time. Picture the reaction of the friends afterwards. Whose financial advisor takes clients and their friends to a rock concert?! It's perfectly acceptable to do something you enjoy with other people. This allows you to connect with them in a genuine way. Chris expands here on how he and his staff maximize experiences for their clients.

"The key thing is to try and understand what interests our clients have," he says. "What we've done is simply ask them about the things they like to do. These might include a wine tasting dinner or going out for a more personalized dinner experience, going to New York Yankee games, Carolina Hurricanes games. We really try to get a good feel for what motivates them and tie into that."

Not only do Chris and his team invite clients to their favorite events, they create an overall experience, complete with fun takeaways. Prior to concerts they provide food and drinks for a tail-gate party. They develop their branding by giving clients golf shirts or cocktail glasses with their name and logo.

The magic is in customizing your approach to your clients. Brainstorm five things you enjoy doing and would be open to doing with clients. Add another list for your best clients and five things they enjoy doing, too. If you are going to coordinate an event that makes a Wow! impression with your best client, choose an activity off your mutual lists—not because you have to, or should, but because you know you would both enjoy the activity.

Want to add more of a hook? Bring people into a place they don't normally have access to. Exclusivity wins! Maybe it's a country club or social club, a business club, a luxury box at a concert or sporting event, immediate seating at the best or latest hot restaurant in town. *What will attract people to attend your event?* Think exclusivity.

How will people learn about your event? Think about the last big blockbuster movie you saw. How did you find out about it? Probably from multiple sources. The greater the "buzz" before a movie release, the larger the revenue on opening weekend. Your events might not enjoy a blockbuster movie marketing budget, but you can learn from their strategies. Use multiple approaches to create awareness to your targeted invitees. This could include an intriguing invitation through the mail, an email, a new website, a phone call, a referral through someone else or directly in person.

You want your invitation to be unique and stand out. Drew Watson, a CFP from Kentucky, is in the top 1 percent of financial advisors nationally. For one of Drew's retirement events, he sent a branded key in a gift-wrapped jewelry box. The message with it said "The key to your retirement, more to come…"

Here's the thought process behind Drew's strategy. "We try to be very creative," he says. "You have to know the audience. If the audience is feminine, offer something that will appeal to them. For example, if it is a traditional family and the wife gets the mail, send something nicely wrapped and create buzz that way. We also created some suspense by sending out non-letterhead envelopes saying 'be on the lookout, you're going to get a really nice package in the mail.'"

Sometimes businesses invite people to events with a ho-hum invitation in the mail. When people don't show up, they excuse themselves, saying, "These events don't work where I live." In the majority of situations, however, that's not true. A personal introduction, made either over the phone or, preferably, in person. will significantly boost the number of people who attend your events. Start with a very personal invitation and then build from there. Surround that invitation with your own version of a blockbuster movie launch.

My team doesn't stop with the personal invitation and surround-sound awareness campaign, though. I have developed a specific process to boost the attendance and results for the events I hold in my practice. Many of the professionals I work with have implemented the same systems and have seen a significant boost in their results with new clients.

When it comes to the logistics of event planning, it is vital to have a person who is gifted at coordination. That may be you at the beginning, but eventually you will have to delegate those responsibilities. Having a talented planner in place is especially important for a new event or an event that is being held at a new venue.

If you are handling these tasks right now, here are some tips to remember. Always remember that the people who work at your venue might have a different idea about how your event should go than you do. There are extra considerations when you hold an educational event at a nicer restaurant. The restaurant's goal is to build an eating experience that will probably not be over within sixty minutes. However, a five course meal might not work if there is going to be an educational component for a larger group. Sometimes you are faced with the opposite dilemma: maybe you want to provide a longer dining experience, but the restaurant is trying to push you out on a busy night to sit another party at your table.

Work ahead (preparation) and explain to your venue managers exactly what you want, and do so well-ahead of the event. Remember to have this conversation with the staff person in charge of the dining room that night, not just with the person you booked the event with.

When you arrive (early!) to the event, immediately talk with the staff and explain your timing and goals. Give specific timeframes and instructions. Over the years, I have spoken at hundreds of events in my own practice and for other financial advisors—*the top influence on results was how well the venue was able to perform!* If they capably executed my instructions, we enjoyed the top results in the country. If they did not execute exactly what I wanted, the results were handicapped.

The suggestions in this chapter are meant to tickle your brain and make you think about your clients and how you interact with them. Maybe taking a client to a rock concert isn't in your comfort zone, but you have a staff member who can track down an autographed album that you can share with that client over dinner. The key is knowing your clients and their passions and then customizing your connection with them.

CHAPTER 7: MARKETING MIND-SET REVIEW

1. Find events that will appeal to both you and the new people you want to connect with. What will intrigue clients and potential new prospects?

2. Consider venue. Where will people want to go? Overcome a prospect's fear of a hard sell by offering your event at an exclusive place they don't normally have access to.

3. Pay attention to how you invite people to your events. Personal invitations mean the most; don't just mail an invitation. Learn from the launch of a blockbuster movie—use different outlets to maximize awareness. Use a booster confirmation courtesy call to paint the picture for what will happen when your guest arrives, instead of just calling to confirm.

4. Prepare ahead of time. Explain to your venue managers what you want to have happen—this can make or break your events.

EXERCISE #7 – PREPARATION SYSTEM BUILDER

- *What activities do your best clients and prospects enjoy?*

- *Where would they want to go? Can you think of a place they can't say no to if invited?*

- *List five strategies that will help you create awareness around your events beyond the invitation.*

- *Create a timeline for those strategies.*

FOLLOW-UP BREEDS TRUST — TRUST EQUALS SUCCESS

There is an important relationship between follow up and trust—too many businesses and people neglect this dynamic. The key to follow up is building a system and implementing it. The biggest difference between a bull and a bear is that bears hibernate. *Don't hibernate when you need to follow up!*

Most business owners do not have a great follow-up system because they are caught up in the pressure of their day-to-day operations. This is how you can be unique and build trust right from the start. People immediately sense a difference when timely follow-up is implemented and your intentions to support them are clear. This difference is the beginning of a path to trust—a path I believe in.

"Jon is extremely deliberate about who he wants to be and what value he wants to bring to the world, whether that's in his practice or his coaching work," says Bill Williams, executive vice-president of Ameriprise. "What's interesting about Jon is that you never have the sense that he's in it for himself or to make money. He's in it to make a difference in the world."

If you follow through on everything in this book but don't follow up with your clients, you can't make a positive difference and your efforts will be erased! A business owner's mind tends to move quickly, sometimes leaving small items in the dust. However, follow-up is not a small item.

The success of my practice in attracting more clients is largely due to the follow-up system we have refined over the years. It has been molded from our experiences and the experiences of the many coaching clients I have the privilege of working with. I have seen many businesses implement my systems and then enjoy significant boosts in their new client acquisition. We've been intentional about our follow-up and protective of the trust we enjoy from our clients.

Follow-up is about building on the next interaction points and keeping *you* at the forefront with others. You may connect with people when you originally meet, but it may not be enough for them to go deeper with you or, more importantly, to do business with you. Successful businesses require their clients to build up a significant level of trust before they even engage to do business. The process of building trust involves engaging in a relationship with prospects who learn more about you and genuinely like you.

Sandra Price is an advisor who establishes trust and takes follow-up to new levels. One of her clients was intimidated by the car-buying process. This came up in a conversation with Sandra after the client's husband had died. They were discussing problems the woman was having with the car, and Sandra suggested it was time to buy a new one. Beyond the emotional challenge of giving up what had been her husband's car, the woman admitted she had never bought a car before and was intimidated by the process.

During the next few weeks, Sandra walked through the process with her and helped her research vehicle information, accompanied her to the dealership, and supported her during the negotiation process.

"What's unique about what we do is that we have a very concierge style of service we provide to our clients," Sandra says. "Really, we take the financial planning to the 'nth' degree. Everything we do from events to how we engage with people is personalized to who they are and what they need."

This heightened level of client service sets Sandra's practice apart, but early on she also recognized the need for a mind-set shift from being a financial advisor to being the CEO/President of a business. Part of that mind-set involved never underestimating the role she and her team play in a client's life.

"In our business, we learned from Jon the value of what we bring to the client," she says. "It's not tangible in many ways. The true philosophy of financial planning is not something you can always see on the page. I've learned to respect that through our work with Jon and his team."

Why is follow-up so integral to our professional success? Because the excitement and pleasure of meeting someone new has the potential to wear off quickly. It is important to initiate follow-up items almost immediately after the first interaction. Vary the touches and communications to remain at the forefront of a client's mind without appearing anxious or overbearing. Don't say "when can we get together again?" Instead, ask about things you know they like or topics you have in common.

The best marketers find reasons to connect with their prospects. It might be setting up the next meeting, doing something fun together, enjoying a meal, or just having coffee to keep an interaction going. The key here is not to pursue; instead invite them to do something with you.

If there is an activity you know they enjoy (because they told you and you listened when you met them), invite them to that activity with you. Create a reason for them to want to participate in your next interaction. Here's a good model to follow: set the next interaction during your time together. This eliminates the chance of the business owner forgetting or the follow-up disappearing along with any memory of you.

Your follow-up system should include a checklist of everything that needs to happen, from the first engagement of a top prospect to the point where the prospect becomes a top client. Incorporate this list into a contact management system (like ACT! by Sage, for example) with reminders to help make sure these items are executed. Assigning a staff person to execute these items increases the likelihood of the tasks being completed.

Delivering different follow-up items will help differentiate you from your competition. Handwritten notes, personal calls, and even gifts can be another difference maker for you. In my office, we have a regular prospect follow-up checklist and an elite prospect checklist. Elite prospects will usually receive small gifts on occasion. We use free or more cost-effective communications for our regular prospects.

Gifts do not have to be extravagant or expensive, just relevant. When you listen and learn about people, you can use this information to help select the gift. There is a top practice in North Carolina that will select and send a complimentary book that matches the prospect. Others send articles about a discussion topic. Follow up if there is an upcoming event or special communication about an issue your client is interested in.

Most professionals worry that they will be perceived as pursuing a prospect too strongly, and as a result, do not follow up nearly enough. This is a mistake. On average, professionals will follow up with prospects only twice when it takes an average of about eight contact points for them to engage in the next steps with you. Be sure there are enough touch points built into your system, and that the communications are varied.

Ongoing touches with existing clients and prospects help keep you at the top of their minds. These touches can include communications on a regular schedule, like an emailed newsletter or a blog post. The internet offers you a venue to send cost-effective, prewritten, and automated email. Your expertise should be posted in concise fashion. Include updates, tips, or just a related story that people will enjoy reading.

Email communications should be short and sweet. Put your message in the subject line so people can easily see it in their inbox—the shortest, easiest responses are typically the ones that people respond to first. My regular communications to both prospects and clients usually look similar. They receive a monthly email and a quarterly hard-copy newsletter in the mail. Prospects and connectors also receive invitations to my events and webinars. These invitations are not long or detailed. Instead, we ship them so that my name appears in their inbox and keeps thoughts of my practice current.

Facebook and LinkedIn are two additional online media formats that allow you to connect with more people and create additional awareness. When you post regular updates, you put your name in front of people more often! But remember: the updates should include positive and inspiring messages for the reader—not what you ate for breakfast. One post example might read: *"Watched a client celebrate early retirement today. It is so much fun helping people."*

Once a client is with a firm, there is more pain in moving than staying. For your prospects who are affiliated with someone else, the challenge is to help them overcome the pain of parting with your competition. The follow-up contact with these prospects will look different than the follow-up for regular or elite prospects or existing clients. It requires a careful strategy, and this is an area where I help top advisors and business owners align with best practices and build a unique process that works for them.

Remember, the follow-up system is a long-term strategy that works well for people who are not quite ready to do business with you yet and for people you have been doing business with for years. People have different needs at different times. When you keep your name in the inbox of that prospect you met two years ago, chances are he will turn to you when the need arises for your services. Always be intentional about your follow-up with both your existing clients and your potential prospects. You may not go car-shopping with them every time, but the difference in focus will amaze them—and you. *Don't be a bear and hibernate with your follow-up; be a bull and make it happen!*

CHAPTER 8: MARKETING MIND-SET REVIEW

1. Build a checklist so follow-up items do not fall through the cracks.

2. Leverage technology and staff to create reminders for follow-up items and execute them.

3. Handwritten notes are a lost art form—be different.

4. Intrigue prospects by using customized gifts that are relevant to them.

5. Ongoing and even automated "touch" communications help keep you in the network of potential prospects and existing clients.

6. When someone needs your services, will they think of you or someone else?

EXERCISE #8 – FOLLOW-UP SYSTEM BUILDER

What items do you want to be part of your follow-up system?

Build your eight- to ten-step follow-up system and be sure to set yourself apart from the others in your industry.

New Follow-Up System

-

-

-

-

-

-

-

-

-

-

Touch System Builder

- *How often will your ongoing touches go out?*

- *How will you manage your list of recipients?*

- *How can you automate your ongoing touch system?*

PLAN FOR SUCCESS

"If you don't know where you are going,
you will end up somewhere else."
Yogi Berra

You have the power to determine where you want to go personally and professionally. You can do this under the trained guidance of a professional coach—who accelerates your results and success by making sure you are focused and are held accountable. But even if you don't utilize the services of a coach, you need to create a vision of your success.

That's why I wrote this book—so that you will identify and build upon your vision. Recognizing and executing your vision will help you make better decisions. Use words and images to help you remember what you want for yourself and your business. Successful business owners build a collage of these words and images and keep them in a place where they will be reminded of their vision every day.

When you commit to aligning everyday decisions with your vision of where you want to go you will achieve your goals faster. Here's what happened to me:

- The first year I built my vision, I accomplished all of my annual goals in the first six months of the year.

- The next year, I accomplished all of my annual goals in just over three months.

This is not about me; it is about the power of visioning and the path to bigger and better results. When you combine visioning with a well-thought-out marketing plan and practical follow-up strategies, there is no goal out of reach.

"I've seen Jon help people—he's adept in areas where a lot of financial advisors have problems, like client acquisition, technical savvy—bringing people up to speed," says Drew Watson. "Jon is a great person to bring in for those types of problems. He does a great job with staff. He's a solid individual. He's very authentic. He is and does what he says he's going to do. He's not going to come in and do anything that is not going to help an advisee."

Here's why vision alignment is used in so many coaching models: over time, you train your brain to think about the vision unconsciously. Just like building a muscle, you have to work at it. The more you do the work, the more successful you become! I have seen this work over and over with the clients I coach.

When you continually reflect on your vision, imagining the person you want to be and the business you want to have, the more this vision will take precedence in your thoughts as you make decisions. This also serves as a warning flag when you make decisions that may be out of alignment with your goals and vision. Those decisions won't look or feel right.

As you build your vision and outline your marketing goals, consider the importance of planning for client acquisition in advance. When you are intentional about acquiring new clients, you have a greater chance of succeeding. You don't need to wave a magic marketing wand to acquire new clients. Instead, you have to pay attention to the basics.

- Reveal the value you offer to prospects.

- Target your efforts for results.

- Use your connectors to gain referrals.

- Duplicate your best clients through referrals.

- Meet people—personally, professionally, casually.

- Find common connections during those meetings.

- Offer people a Wow! experience they will keep talking about.

- Pay attention to event logistics when you offer an event for prospects.

- Engage in daily levels of marketing.

- Implement a formal follow-up system for regular and elite prospects as well as your existing clients.

"The first thing I like about Jon is that he does what he says he's going to do," says financial advisor Chris Murphy. "His follow-up is strong, which is very important to me. I don't fall off the radar screen. With Jon, that just doesn't happen. He calls in and says he wants to talk about this and that. He understands the big picture and why it's important to make sure the appropriate actions are taken."

The big picture that some people tend to neglect includes daily marketing. Stay with me here: this is a simple concept, but too many business owners tread water in their day-to-day activities, which limits their marketing potential. Here's the key: prioritize your marketing activities if you want to attract more clients.

Travis Chaney notes that too many business professionals are afraid of rejection, but that's no excuse to avoid marketing your services:

"At the end of the day you need new assets, new clients in order to grow," he says. "In the financial advisor business, clients leave, clients die, clients take out money for their goals and take out money for their emergencies. When you are an asset-based business and assets are leaving, you must replace them."

Where did your new clients come from in the last two years? Duplicate what has worked for you and your business, but evaluate the following: is there potential to increase the amount and frequency of the activities that are working for you? Is there a good balance between investment and returns?

Look to others as well. Many successful businesses copy best practices from other businesses. What other marketing activities can you add to your mix? Have you shied away from online marketing because you are intimidated and feel out of date? That's fixable.

Also consider what marketing activities you have used in the last two years that yielded limited or no results. These need to be eliminated immediately. Stop using activities that do not work and do not generate desirable new clients. However, the caveat here is "don't discard an approach after the very first try."

Networking is a perfect example of something that takes time to bear fruit. You can't get to know someone who is new to you in one outing. Give it some time and also consider preparing a formal measurement tool. Evaluating if a marketing endeavor can produce future results or is producing no results requires intuition and probably an outside perspective from a coach.

If there is no plan to acquire new clients or, worse, no overall vision plan for the year, then your goals will slip away. Some business owners make excuses for themselves throughout the year, enabling them to delay marketing activities. They can sound so persuasive! Here are some of my favorite excuses that coaching clients have given me in the past:

January is busy because I am kicking off the year.
February is just too cold and people don't want to come out and see me.
March is college basketball tournament time.
April 15 is the tax deadline.
May—everyone is trying to get things done before Memorial Day.
June—summer has officially started so there is not much time for business.
July—this is the busiest vacation month.
August—parents are taking their kids to college.
September—school has started.
October—everyone is going to see the fall foliage.
November starts the holiday season and everyone is busy.
December—Really? We can get started in January.

An entire year of delays, and the delays start over the next year! *Don't let this be you.* There are no bad times of year to market, just myths and excuses.

The most successful marketers avoid delaying activities and results by creating a calendar of the marketing activities they want to execute for the entire year. The events in your mix should be pre-scheduled to make sure they happen. Then you and your team will have time to properly plan and run with your new preparation steps.

Some activities can produce more immediate results, and others lead to results in the future. Check out these examples of each in terms of how quickly you can generate results:

Short-Term Results
Follow up with existing and old prospects.
Go to your connectors and identify more potential prospects.
Go to your best clients and duplicate them.

Mid-Term Results
Organize small or large events to meet new people.

Long-Term Results
Network with individuals on a personal, professional, and casual level.
Build alliances with other professionals.

As a successful business owner, you need to think in terms of investments and returns instead of costs and expenses. This is the greatest difference between top businesses and mediocre wannabes. Every dollar spent within the business is an investment. You make an investment on office space, your people, and yourself.

"One of Jon's strengths is that he invests in himself, which is investing with the people he works with," says Travis Chaney. "He's a great listener. There are times when I call him and he knew it was time to listen instead of just helping. If you're not listening, you're missing the connection you really need to make a difference with that person. If we are listening, the solutions appear so much easier than when we don't listen."

Marketing is no different—there are investments and potential returns. Be smart with your investments. If you have a great opportunity, make an investment in capturing it! Avoid business investments that will not yield you a tangible return.

This book is designed to be a call to action. Marketing Action! If you want different results, you need to do something different.

You live in the perfect environment. There is no greater investment than in business, and there is no better place to do it than America. The most profitable and successful business owners do the strategies outlined in this book—you can do it too!

Have you stepped away from the stationary bike and moved into a positive mind-set about marketing your business? Are you considering using a coach for the extra help you need to envision and reach your goals? Leverage the people around you and find someone you trust to hold you accountable. For many successful business owners, coaching is the key to moving forward with purpose and results.

I'm delighted to talk with you about exceeding your potential and how to tackle the slopes of success. In the meantime, you can seize the moment and start the process by implementing two items from this book in the next week. Then add one more next week and another the week after next.

If you are serious about achieving your growth goals and overall success as soon as possible, let's see if an in-depth coaching relationship is right for you. Transform to a new and improved mind-set. Tailor a customized action plan and be prepared to experience real results like the real people highlighted throughout this book.

What are you waiting for? Jump on that racing bike, and let's head for the Alps!

Send me an email at <u>jon@dynamicdirections-d2.com</u> *and let me know how it goes!*

Sample Marketing Plan Components

1.   Immediate Opportunity List

Touch base with your connectors. *Who are they?*
Duplicate your best clients. *Who are they?*
Reconnect with hot prospects. *Who are they?*

2. **Marketing activities for the year**

    Smaller and targeted activities
    Networking events
    Unique events

3. **Other opportunities**

    Network with professionals and build alliances. *Who will you target?*
    Complete a marketing calendar for the year.
    Determine investments and potential returns of your marketing budget.

SCHEDULE WEEKLY TIME TO WORK ON MARKETING!

CHAPTER 9: MARKETING MIND-SET REVIEW

1. Don't let myths or excuses hold you back from executing marketing activities.

2. Schedule your activities and events in advance.

3. Know how quickly to expect results from different marketing strategies.

4. Build your components into a magnetic marketing plan..

EXERCISE #9 – CREATE A VISION OF YOUR NEW MARKETING PLAN

What Do You Want?

Why do you do what you do?

What do you want for yourself from your business?

What do you want for your business?

How will you be aware of these over time?

How will you use this information to influence your decision making?

Identify your investment for marketing and client acquisition.

What is your expected return on this investment?

When will your activities take place? Build a marketing calendar with all of your activities for the next year.

How could a coach help you accelerate your results?

Made in the USA
Monee, IL
31 January 2020